POPULATI
AND COMMUNITIES

Life Science

A **population** is all the living things of the same kind that live in the same place.

A **community** is all the populations that live in an ecosystem at the same time.

Science Vocabulary
community [kuh•MYOO•nuh•tee]
population [pop•yuh•LAY•shun]

desert
[DEZ•ert]

ecosystem
[EE•koh•sis•tuhm]

a very dry place that gets very little rain

all the living and nonliving things in an area

group
[GROOP]

a number of people, animals, or things together

living
[LIV•ing]

things that are alive

meerkat
[MEER•kat]

a small desert mammal

ocean
[OH•shuhn]

a large body of salt water

rain forest
[RAYN FAWR•ist]

a place with many tall trees that gets lots of rain

turtle
[TER•tl]

a reptile with a large shell covering its body

POPULATIONS

Populations are *groups* of *living* things that are the same and live in the same place. A group of people who live in the same place is a population.

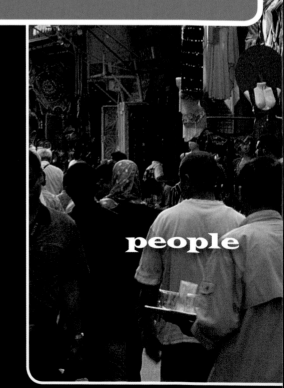

people

The people who live in this town are its population.

tree

A group of bees that live in the same place is a population.

Populations of bees can live in trees.

Populations of bees can live in beehives.

bee population

bees

beekeeper

beehives

A beekeeper checks out the bee population.

A group of plants that are the same
and live in the same place is a population.
This is a population of fir trees.

tree population

fir trees

snow

Fir trees can live in a place where it snows.

birds

COMMUNITIES

A *community* is all the populations that live in the same place.

A town is a community of all the living things that live there.

Key

P = populations

dogs

cats

P trees

P people

People, cats, dogs, birds, and trees
are populations that live in this town.

dolphins

An *ocean* is a community
of all the living things that live there.
Turtles live in the ocean.
The turtle population
is part of the ocean's community.

Key

 = populations

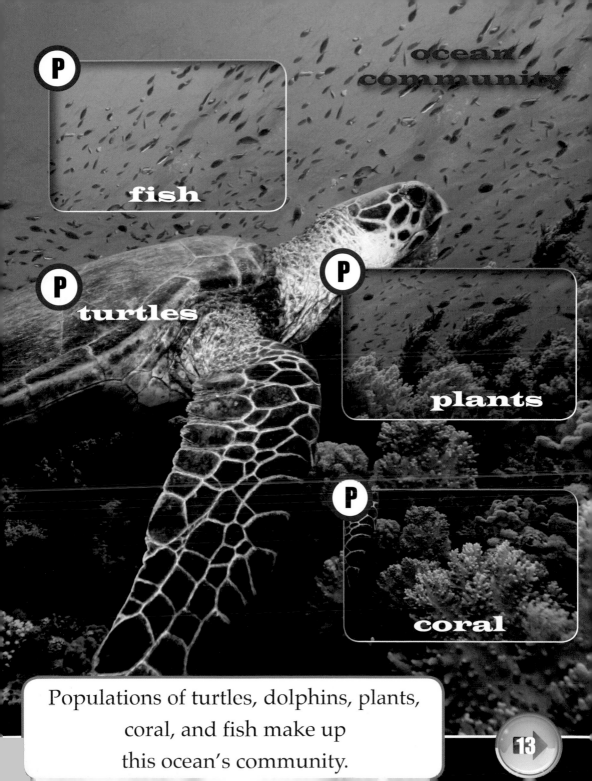

P fish

ocean community

P turtles

P plants

P coral

Populations of turtles, dolphins, plants, coral, and fish make up this ocean's community.

P trees

A *desert* is a community
of all the living things that live there.
Meerkats live in the desert.
The meerkat population
is part of the desert's community.

Key

P = populations

P birds

desert community

P meerkats

P people

P insects

These populations are part of the Kalahari Desert community.

COMMUNITIES AND ECOSYSTEMS

Communities may not live

in the same part of the *ecosystem*.

A pond community

lives in different parts of a pond.

Different populations live above, on,

and under the water.

A kingfishers

O **U** frogs

Key

A = above

O = on

U = under

A dragonflies

O ducks

water

O water lilies

U fish

bats

A *rain-forest* community

lives in different parts of a rain forest.

Some populations live above the rain forest.

Some populations live in the trees.

Some populations live on the forest floor.

Key

E = emergent layer

C = canopy

U = understory

F = forest floor

F moss

F

anteaters

rain forest ecosystem

E birds

E C butterflies

C trees monkeys

U sloths

U F snakes

log

F ferns

F ants

Concept Web

A concept web is a way of showing related things.

This concept web shows you some populations related to a pond community.
This concept web uses words.

kingfishers

waterlilies

Pond Community

fish

ducks

frogs

Concept Chart

A concept chart, like a concept web, is a way of showing related things.

This chart shows some animals that make up a desert community.
This chart uses photos.

Desert
Community

Science Concepts: Populations and Communities

Populations are groups of living things that are the same and live in the same place.

All the populations that live in an ecosystem at the same time, form a community.

All members of a community live in the same ecosystem.

Communities do not all have to live in the same part of an ecosystem.